Try CGP's bite-sized SPaG ~~bol~~ tests!

Short bursts of regular practice can really help pupils master grammar, punctuation and spelling for the KS2 SATS. That's why we've made this terrific book of 10-Minute Tests.

They're just like mini versions of the real SATS — but with puzzles and handy scoresheets added in as a bonus.

We've even included pull-out scripts for each spelling test, with the full audio files downloadable from:

www.cgpbooks.co.uk/KS210MinTests

What CGP is all about

Our sole aim here at CGP is to produce the highest quality books — carefully written, immaculately presented and dangerously close to being funny.

Then we work our socks off to get them out to you — at the cheapest possible prices.

Contents

Set A

Grammar & Punctuation Test 1 2
Grammar & Punctuation Test 2 6
Grammar & Punctuation Test 3 10
Grammar & Punctuation Test 4 14
Spelling Test 18
Puzzle 19
Scoresheet 20

Set B

Grammar & Punctuation Test 1 21
Grammar & Punctuation Test 2 25
Grammar & Punctuation Test 3 29
Grammar & Punctuation Test 4 33
Spelling Test 37
Puzzle 38
Scoresheet 39

Set C

Grammar & Punctuation Test 1 40

Grammar & Punctuation Test 2 44

Grammar & Punctuation Test 3 48

Grammar & Punctuation Test 4 52

Spelling Test 56

Puzzle 57

Scoresheet 58

Hints and Tips 59

Answers 60

Progress Chart 70

The transcripts for the spelling tests can be found in a pull-out section in the middle of the book, or you can use the online audio files.

Published by CGP

Editors: Emma Bonney, Joe Brazier, Emma Crighton, Heather Gregson, Lucy Loveluck, Heather McClelland
With thanks to Holly Poynton for the proofreading.

ISBN: 978 1 78294 238 2
Clipart from Corel®
Printed by Elanders Ltd, Newcastle upon Tyne.
Based on the classic CGP style created by Richard Parsons.

Text, design, layout and original illustrations © Coordination Group Publications Ltd. (CGP) 2019
All rights reserved.

Photocopying this book is not permitted, even if you have a CLA licence.
Extra copies are available from CGP with next day delivery • 0800 1712 712 • www.cgpbooks.co.uk

Set A: Grammar & Punctuation 1

There are **11 questions** in this test. Give yourself **10 minutes** to answer them all.

1. Which of the events below is the **most** likely to happen?

   tick **one** box

   We will go to the cinema tonight. ☐
   He might go bowling with me. ☐
   She could teach me how to dance. ☐
   They can tell us the story later. ☐

   1 mark

2. In the sentence below, Louise told her dad about going to the park before she went.
   Write the correct **verb form** in the space to complete the sentence.

   Louise .... told her dad she was going to the park, so he wasn't surprised when she went.

   1 mark

3. Read the sentences below.
   Tick **two** sentences that are grammatically correct.

   tick **two** boxes

   Remember to buy a ticket before you got on the train. ☐
   I bought a hat, but I didn't bought a dress. ☐
   We cooked curry for tea, and we baked a cake for dessert. ☐
   They will tell us a story, and we will listen carefully. ☐

   1 mark

Set A: Grammar & Punctuation 1

4. Draw a line to match each sentence with the most likely final **punctuation mark**. You can only use each punctuation mark **once**.

Get out of the house	.
Where are my trainers	?
It is half past ten in the morning	!

1 mark

5. Put a letter in each box to show which **word class** the words belong to.

| determiner A | noun B | adjective C | verb D |

He used to love those sour sweets.
    ↑   ↑   ↑   ↑
   □   □   □   □

1 mark

6. Read the sentences below.
Tick the sentence which uses **commas** correctly.

tick **one** box

Even after all this time, I still don't like cabbage. □
Even after, all this time I still don't like cabbage. □
Even after all this time I still, don't like cabbage. □
Even after all this, time I still don't like cabbage. □

1 mark

7. Complete the table below by writing a suitable **synonym** or **antonym** in each empty box.

Word	Synonym	Antonym
intelligent	clever	foolish
optimistic		pessimistic
courteous	polite	
vibrant	lively	

2 marks

8. Read the sentence below and underline the **subordinating conjunction**.

Although it is really late, I can't get to sleep.

1 mark

9. Tick **one** box to show which word in the sentence below is an **adverb**.

I've never seen a racing car that can grow wings and fly away.

 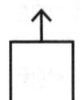

1 mark

10. Add **punctuation** to the sentence below so that it is correct.

    The teacher asked his pupils Is Marcus ill today

    1 mark

11. Put a tick in each row of the table below to show whether the words in bold are a **main clause** or a **subordinate clause**.

Sentence	Main clause	Subordinate clause
When Ryan arrives tomorrow, we'll go to the cinema.		
Dad says that if we're good, **we can buy some popcorn**.		
Ryan, **who's my cousin**, loves popcorn.		

1 mark

END OF TEST

/ 12

Set A: Grammar & Punctuation 2

There are **11 questions** in this test. Give yourself **10 minutes** to answer them all.

1. Read the sentences below and underline all the **conjunctions**.

   We went outside after it had stopped raining.

   I'm not going to the party unless Naomi comes with me.

   Whenever Jimmy's dog barks, his cat hides under the bed.

   1 mark

2. Read the sentence below.
   Using the verb in the brackets, complete the sentence in the **present progressive** tense.

   I .... a biscuit.   (to eat)

   1 mark

3. The children ignored the alarm.

   Rewrite the active sentence above in the **passive** form.

   ....

   ....

   1 mark

4. Tick the sentence which uses brackets correctly.

tick **one** box

(Graham my uncle) loves smoked salmon. ☐

Graham my uncle (loves smoked) salmon. ☐

Graham (my uncle loves) smoked salmon. ☐

Graham (my uncle) loves smoked salmon. ☐

1 mark

5. Circle the **object** in the sentence below.

Mrs Patel bought a pastry.

1 mark

6. Tick **two** boxes to show which of the words in the sentence below are **relative pronouns**.

The woman, who was very tall, had forgotten to bring her screwdriver, which meant she couldn't hang up our pictures.

1 mark

7. Read the words below.
   Tick the word which is an **adjective** made by adding a suffix to the word **'cheer'**.

   tick **one** box

   cheer**fully** ☐
   cheer**s** ☐
   cheer**ful** ☐
   cheer**er** ☐

   1 mark

8. Tick **one** box to show which word is an **adverb**.

   Marcus swung the bat and hit the ball forcefully.

   1 mark

9. Read the sentence below.
   Underline the longest possible noun phrase.

   In our garage, there's a brightly coloured, ultrafast sports car.

   1 mark

10. Read the sentence below and underline the **subordinate clause**.

I don't eat tomatoes unless they're cooked.

1 mark

11. My dads house isnt far away so Im often there to see him.

a) Circle the **three** words in the sentence above that need an **apostrophe**.

b) Pick one of the words that you have circled. Explain why it needs an apostrophe.

Word chosen ....

....

....

2 marks

END OF TEST

/ 12

Set A: Grammar & Punctuation 3

There are **11 questions** in this test. Give yourself **10 minutes** to answer them all.

1. Circle the **determiner** in each of the sentences below.

   Whose pencil case is it?

   Please take off your shoes.

   Harry took an easy exam.

   Ron came last in every race.

   1 mark

2. Read the sentences below.
   Tick the **two** sentences which are most likely to end with an **exclamation mark**.

	tick **two** boxes
Our house is slightly chilly in winter	☐
What an incredible goal that was	☐
I think Petra is a finalist this year	☐
Do you have a lot of homework	☐
Get out of my way	☐

   1 mark

3. Circle the correct form of the **verb** in brackets to complete each sentence using Standard English.

   Tomek (was / were) the best at playing the recorder.

   We (was / were) allowed to meet the band backstage.

   I (was / were) doing my homework when he arrived.

   1 mark

4. To do her experiment, Nicola needs a microwave, a thermometer and a bar of chocolate.
   Write what Nicola needs as a list of **bullet points** on the lines below. Remember to punctuate your answer correctly.

   For the experiment, Nicola will need:

   - ....
   - ....
   - ....

   1 mark

5. Read the sentence below and underline the **relative clause**.

   Amar met Laura, who is now his best friend, last July.

   1 mark

6. Circle the **adverbial phrase** in the sentence below.

   A new teacher joined our school this term.

   1 mark

7. Tick the sentence which uses a **dash** correctly.

   tick **one** box

   Mum found the — car keys they were in her pocket. ☐
   Mum found the car keys — they were in her pocket. ☐
   Mum found the car keys they were in her — pocket. ☐
   Mum found — the car keys they were in her pocket. ☐

   1 mark

8. Circle the **adverb** in each of the sentences below.

   Sasha will probably teach you to paint.

   The biscuits will run out soon.

   1 mark

9. Read the words below. Tick the option that describes what the root 'cent' means in this word family.

   century   percentage   centipede

   tick **one** box

   smell   ☐
   hundred ☐
   part   ☐
   insect   ☐

   1 mark

10. The sentence below is missing a **semi-colon**.
Tick **one** box to show where the semi-colon should go.

Marie is in hospital she's having an operation.
☐ ☐ ☐

1 mark

11. Write a sensible **question** to fit each answer in the table below.
One has already been done for you.

Question	Answer
Where do you live?	At 42 Lime Tree Avenue.
	A sandwich and a banana.
	At quarter to nine.

2 marks

END OF TEST

/ 12

Set A: Grammar & Punctuation 4

There are **12 questions** in this test. Give yourself **10 minutes** to answer them all.

1. Read the sentence below and circle the word or words that make it a **question**.

   You're not allergic to nuts , are you ?

   1 mark

2. Draw a line to match each **prefix** with the most likely root word. One has already been done for you.

   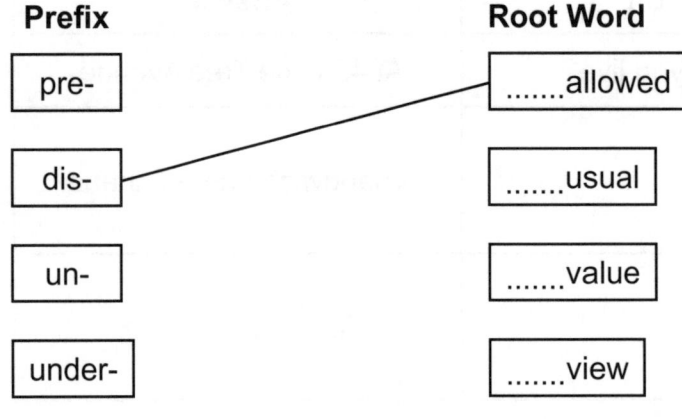

   1 mark

3. Tick the sentence which uses an **apostrophe** correctly.

   tick **one** box

   The cherrie's stalks have been removed. ☐

   I think this is the mices' hole. ☐

   Everyone's costumes are over there. ☐

   1 mark

4. Read the sentences below.
   Tick the **two** sentences which are **statements**.

   tick **two** boxes

   Yasmin offered me a sweet. ☐

   Where is the nearest airport? ☐

   Don't touch that! ☐

   Would you like to go to the zoo? ☐

   My favourite colour is orange. ☐

   1 mark

5. Read the two sentences below. Explain how the **comma** changes the meaning.

   Will you remember to pay, Jane?
   Will you remember to pay Jane?

   ....

   ....

   ....

   1 mark

6. Read the sentence below.
   Choose **conjunctions** from the box to complete the sentence.
   You can only use each conjunction **once**.

   | before | but | because |

   I lost the board game .... I lost at cards,

   .... it didn't matter .... I won at chess.

   1 mark

7. Read the sentences below. Tick the sentence which should be written as two separate **sentences**.

tick **one** box

I love strawberries, but I hate raspberries. ☐

Charlie lives with Sam, Millie and George. ☐

I heard you were ill are you feeling better? ☐

We didn't go to school because of the snow. ☐

1 mark

8. Read the sentence below. Circle the most suitable **relative pronoun** to complete the sentence.

I'm so pleased for the team .... won the tournament.

whom   when   whose   that

1 mark

9. Read the sentence below. Replace the word in bold with a **more formal** word. Write the word in the box.

Put an extra jumper on — it's a bit **nippy** outside.

☐

1 mark

10. Add a **comma** in the correct place in the sentence below.

Last night Jacob's dad bought us all pizza .

1 mark

11. There is one error in the sentence below.
    Write the **correction** in the box.

    Frances haven't fed the fish today.

    [   ]

    1 mark

12. Put a tick in the correct column to show whether each sentence is **active** or **passive**. One has already been done for you.

Sentence	Active	Passive
Everyone loved watching sports day.	✓	
I was driven here by my mum.		
I can grow fruit and vegetables.		
We were shown round by the tour guide.		

1 mark

END OF TEST

/ 12

Set A: Spelling Test

For this test, you'll need someone to **read out** the transcript from the middle of the book, or you can use the **online audio file**. The test will take about 10 minutes.

mark box

1. The cake .... had been ruined. ☐

2. Matt .... agreed to part with his teddy bear. ☐

3. Emily hates .... , but she loves cycling. ☐

4. The classroom was in complete .... ☐

5. All the .... in the road look lovely. ☐

6. Your .... is grumbling very loudly. ☐

7. It was a great .... that everyone got home safe and sound. ☐

8. There was no .... about who won the race. ☐

9. The .... biscuits are everyone's favourite. ☐

10. He cannot get the .... out of his head. ☐

11. The .... needed repairing urgently. ☐

12. There's a .... between winning and losing. ☐

/ 12

Set A: Spelling Test   © CGP — not to be photocopied

Set A: Puzzle

This puzzle is a brilliant way to practise your grammar skills.

Paige's Puzzle

Paige has hidden the name of her favourite type of word in this crossword. Use the clues below to complete the crossword, then unscramble the letters in the white squares to find out Paige's favourite type of word.

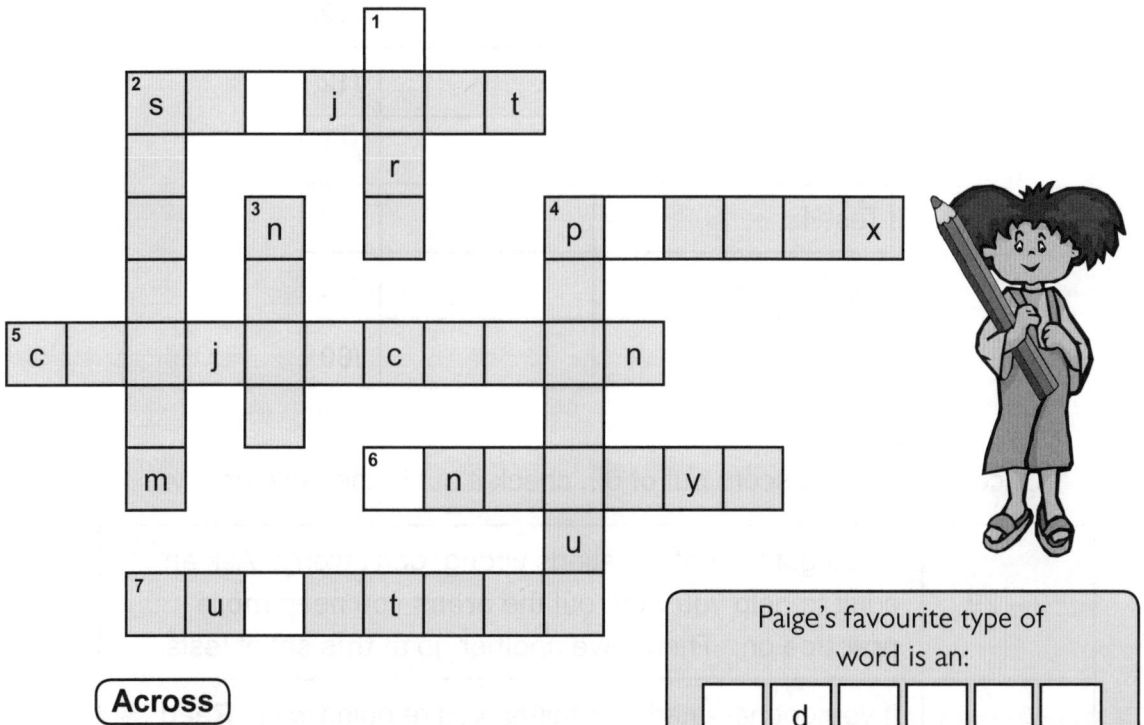

Paige's favourite type of word is an: _ d _ _ _

Across

2. The person or thing that does an action in a sentence.
4. A group of letters that can be added to the start of a word.
5. A word that connects two sentences or clauses.
6. A word that means the opposite of another word.
7. A type of sentence used when you want to ask something.

Down

1. A doing or being word.
2. A word that means the same as another word.
3. A word that names something.
4. Words like 'she' and 'we' that can replace nouns in a sentences.

End of Set A: Scoresheet

You've finished a full set of tests — well done!

Now it's time to put your scores in here
and see how you're getting on.

	Score	
Test 1		/12
Test 2		/12
Test 3		/12
Test 4		/12
Spelling Test		/12
Total		/60

Once you've got a score out of 60, check it out in the table below...

0 – 29	If you got a lot of questions wrong, don't worry. Ask an adult to help you work out the **areas** you need **more practice** on. Then have another go at **this** set of tests.
30 – 45	If you got half-marks or better, you're doing well. **Read** back over your **incorrect** answers and make sure you know **why** they're wrong. Then try the **next set** of tests.
46 – 60	Woohoo! Now have a go at the **next set** of tests — can you beat your score?

But before you do... bend your brain round this one:

Change one letter at a time to make new words, until you get to the word at the end.
The first step has been done for you.

COST   L O S T   _ _ _ _   _ _ _ _   LANE

Set A: Scoresheet

Set B: Grammar & Punctuation 1

There are **11 questions** in this test. Give yourself **10 minutes** to answer them all.

1. Read the sentence below. Tick the pair of phrases that complete the sentence so that it's in the **past progressive** tense.

   Julie .... her bag whilst Felix .... for the tickets.

   tick **one** box

had packed	will look	☐
was packing	was looking	☐
is packing	had looked	☐
will pack	is looking	☐

   1 mark

2. Theres a spider in Lucys bath, so Ill have to catch it.

   a) Circle **three** words in the sentence above that should have an apostrophe.

   b) Pick **one** of the words that you have circled. Explain why it needs an apostrophe.

   Word chosen ....

   ....

   ....

   2 marks

3. Rewrite the sentence below with the **adverbial** at the beginning. Make sure you use the same words and the correct punctuation.

Vince was five years old when his sister was born.

....

....

1 mark

4. Look at the table below. Change the question into a **command**. Write the command in the right-hand column.

Question	Command
Can you tell me the truth?	

1 mark

5. Read the sentence below.
Circle the most suitable **subordinating conjunction** to complete the sentence.

Freda's hands are cold .... she forgot her mittens.

because   if   that   when

1 mark

6. Add the missing **brackets** to the sentences below so that they are correct.

Mr Hargreaves (our history teacher rides a motorbike to school .

My dress the red one) has got a stain on it .

1 mark

7. Read the sentence below, then circle the two words that are **synonyms** of each other.

Garth cheekily added an extra note to Mum's shopping list because he desperately wanted an additional bag of crisps.

1 mark

8. Tick **two** boxes to show which of the words in the sentence below are **prepositions**.

Melanie carefully put the dishes in the dishwasher after dinner.

1 mark

9. Tick the sentence below that uses **capital letters** and **full stops** correctly.

tick **one** box

Last saturday, I went to. Manchester and saw a show. ☐

last Saturday, I went to Manchester and saw a show. ☐

Last Saturday, I went to Manchester and saw a show. ☐

Last Saturday, i went to Manchester and saw a show ☐

1 mark

10. Tick the correct boxes to show whether the **modal verbs** in the sentences show certainty or possibility.

Sentence	Certainty	Possibility
Julie will write a letter to her brother.		
I may see Thomas next Tuesday.		
He shall see a doctor about his leg.		
We might go on holiday to Florida.		

1 mark

11. Tick the **sentence** below that is in the **subjunctive mood**.

tick **one** box

We were the last ones to arrive at football practice. ☐

If I were you, I'd wear shorts and a T-shirt. ☐

Were you the one who won the prize? ☐

You've upset Finn with what you were talking about. ☐

1 mark

END OF TEST

/ 12

Set B: Grammar & Punctuation 2

There are **12 questions** in this test. Give yourself **10 minutes** to answer them all.

1. Underline the **subject** in each of the sentences below.

   Lydia found a beautiful necklace.

   Last week, I played football in the park.

   At 9 o'clock, the postman delivered the letters.

   1 mark

2. Read the sentence below. Circle the **co-ordinating conjunction** and underline the **subordinating conjunction**.

   Patrick is good at cricket and tennis although he doesn't play very often.

   1 mark

3. There are three dessert choices on a menu: chocolate pudding, fruit tart and ice cream.
   Write the choices as a list of **bullet points** on the lines below.
   Remember to punctuate your answer correctly.

   You may choose from these three desserts:

   • ....

   • ....

   • ....

   1 mark

4. Do you <u>ever</u> regret buying that <u>large</u>, <u>pink</u> handbag, Joanne?

In each row, put a tick to show whether each underlined word is an **adjective** or an **adverb**.

Word	Adjective	Adverb
ever		
large		
pink		

1 mark

5. Read the sentence below and circle the word or words that make it a **question**.

"They don't know who I am, do they?"

1 mark

6. Each of the sentences below is missing a **prefix**. Draw a line to match each sentence with the most likely prefix. One has already been done for you.

Sentence — **Prefix**

They were building a new .... market. ——— super-

The doctor gave me .... biotics. — dis-

She is writing her .... biography. — anti-

The delay put them at a .... advantage. — auto-

1 mark

Set B: Grammar & Punctuation 2 — 26 — © CGP — not to be photocopied

7. Tick the two sentences below that correctly use the **present perfect** tense.

tick **two** boxes

Amy bought some bread. ☐

I have told him the truth. ☐

Kimberly has breaked a window. ☐

A flea has bitten my dog. ☐

1 mark

8. Read the sentences below.
Tick the sentence which is most likely to end with an **exclamation mark**.

tick **one** box

I can't believe it, we've won the competition ☐

The gardener was forty-five years old ☐

Can we go to the park please, mum ☐

Feed the dog before you go to bed ☐

1 mark

9. The sentence below is missing a **comma**.
Tick one box to show where the comma should go.

Ralph has just bought a big red and shiny car.
      ↑   ↑   ↑   ↑
      ☐   ☐   ☐   ☐

1 mark

10. Read the sentence below.
    Which **word class** does the word '**race**' belong to?

    Pupils should not **race** down school corridors.

    tick **one** box

    noun ☐
    verb ☐
    adverb ☐
    determiner ☐

    1 mark

11. The sentence below is missing a **hyphen**.
    Tick one box to show where the hyphen should go.

    We booked an incredible ↑ last ↑ minute ↑ holiday ↑ to Lanzarote.
    ☐ ☐ ☐ ☐

    1 mark

12. Tick the sentence below that uses a **colon** correctly.

    tick **one** box

    We are going to the shop: we have no bread or milk. ☐
    We are going to: the shop we have no bread or milk. ☐
    We are going to the: shop we have no bread or milk. ☐
    We are going to the shop we have no bread: or milk. ☐

    1 mark

END OF TEST

/ 12

Set B: Grammar & Punctuation 2   28   © CGP — not to be photocopied

Set B: Grammar & Punctuation 3

There are **11 questions** in this test. Give yourself **10 minutes** to answer them all.

1. Tick the **suffix** below that could be added to all of these words.

   emotion   fiction   accident

   tick **one** box
   less ☐
   ly   ☐
   al   ☐
   ed   ☐

   _____
   1 mark

2. Each of the sentences below is missing a **verb**.
   Draw a line to match each sentence with the most likely verb.

   Sentence   **Verb**

I'll .... to the cinema today.	go
Yesterday, I .... to the cinema.	going
I'm .... to the cinema tomorrow.	went

   _____
   1 mark

3. Read the sentence below.
   Circle the most suitable **pronoun** to complete the sentence.

   That's not your pencil case — it's ....

   I   me   mine   my

   _____
   1 mark

4. Which sentence must end in a **question mark**?

                                                                            tick **one** box

I have no idea which holiday is the cheapest ☐

She asked him what the time was ☐

Which jumper are you going to wear today ☐

I'm asking you where she is ☐

1 mark

5. Read the sentence below.
Insert **inverted commas** in the correct places so that the sentences are punctuated correctly.

"What were you thinking? asked the chef. You can't make meringue with lavender!

1 mark

6. The sentence below is missing a **dash**.
Tick one box to show where the dash should go.

Sarah looked at me she could tell I wasn't joking.

1 mark

7. Tick the sentence below that uses **determiners** correctly.

tick **one** box

We saw a elephant in Uganda. ☐

There was a incredibly loud bang outside. ☐

Lewis found a famous painting last week. ☐

Captain Red Beard has an gigantic ship. ☐

1 mark

8. Read the sentence below.
Circle the most suitable option to complete the sentence so that it uses the **subjunctive** mood.

If I .... a bit taller, I could reach the top shelf.

was   could be   were   would be

1 mark

9. Tick **two** boxes to show which of the words in the sentence below are **relative pronouns**.

The cloud, which was dark grey, was directly above Fred, who wasn't wearing a raincoat.

1 mark

10. Read the sentence below.
Tick the pair of **pronouns** which best completes the sentence.

Phillip asked me where .... could park but .... didn't know either.

tick **one** box

me	I	☐
they	them	☐
he	I	☐
him	he	☐

1 mark

11. Write your own sentence using the word '**drive**' as a **verb**.
Use correct punctuation in your sentence.

....

Write your own sentence using the word '**drive**' as a **noun**.
Use correct punctuation in your sentence.

....

2 marks

END OF TEST

/ 12

Set B: Grammar & Punctuation 4

There are **11 questions** in this test. Give yourself **10 minutes** to answer them all.

1. Read the words below.
   Tick the word which is a **verb** made by adding a **suffix** to the word **'apology'**.

   tick **one** box

   apolog**etic** ☐
   apolog**ise** ☐
   apolog**ies** ☐
   apolog**etically** ☐

   1 mark

2. Write a **question** beginning with the word given below.

   What ....

   ....

   1 mark

3. Read the sentence below. Tick the pair of phrases that complete the sentence so it's in the **present progressive** tense.

   The acrobats .... carefully on the tightrope whilst the clowns .... sweets into the audience.

   tick **one** box

   will balance   will throw   ☐
   were balancing were throwing   ☐
   had balanced   had thrown   ☐
   are balancing   are throwing   ☐

   1 mark

4. Circle the **passive** sentences below.

Mickey burnt the cakes.

Our decision was made.

The prisoner was captured.

I practise playing the guitar.

1 mark

5. The sentence below is missing two **commas**.
Tick **two** boxes to show where the commas should go.

I missed the parade ☐ the one ☐ on High Street ☐ because ☐ I overslept.

1 mark

6. Choose a suitable conjunction to introduce the **subordinate clause** in this sentence.

I like to read .... I eat my breakfast.

tick **one** box

because ☐
while ☐
although ☐
so ☐

1 mark

Key Stage 2
10-Minute Tests
Spelling Test Transcripts

The spelling tests need to be **read out loud** to the children.

You can read the tests out loud to the children by following the instructions below, or you can play an **audio file** from here:

www.cgpbooks.co.uk/ks210mintests

Each test should take about 10 minutes.

For each test, read out the following instructions, and then answer any questions the children have.

- Listen to the instructions I'm about to give you.
- I'm going to read out twelve sentences. These sentences are printed on your answer page, but each one has a word missing. Listen to the missing word and write it in. Make sure you spell it correctly.
- I will read the word, then read the word within a sentence, then I'll say the word a third time.
- The test will now begin.

Now read the spellings to the children:

- Say the spelling number.
- Say "The word is..."
- Read out the word in its sentence.
- Say "The word is..."
- Pause for at least 12 seconds between each of the spellings.

At the end of each test, read out all 12 sentences again, and give the children time to change their answers if they want to.

When the test is over, say "This is the end of the test."

© CGP — not to be photocopied

Set A: Spelling Questions

Read out the instructions from the **first page** of this pull-out. Then read out the following:

1. Spelling one.
   The word is **mixture**.
   *The cake **mixture** had been ruined.*
   The word is **mixture**.

2. Spelling two.
   The word is **sadly**.
   *Matt **sadly** agreed to part with his teddy bear.*
   The word is **sadly**.

3. Spelling three.
   The word is **running**.
   *Emily hates **running**, but she loves cycling.*
   The word is **running**.

4. Spelling four.
   The word is **disorder**.
   *The classroom was in complete **disorder**.*
   The word is **disorder**.

5. Spelling five.
   The word is **houses**.
   *All the **houses** in the road look lovely.*
   The word is **houses**.

6. Spelling six.
   The word is **stomach**.
   *Your **stomach** is grumbling very loudly.*
   The word is **stomach**.

7. Spelling seven.
   The word is **relief**.
   *It was a great **relief** that everyone got home safe and sound.*
   The word is **relief**.

8. Spelling eight.
   The word is **doubt**.
   *There was no **doubt** about who won the race.*
   The word is **doubt**.

9. Spelling nine.
   The word is **delicious**.
   *The **delicious** biscuits are everyone's favourite.*
   The word is **delicious**.

10. Spelling ten.
    The word is **thought**.
    *He cannot get the **thought** out of his head.*
    The word is **thought**.

11. Spelling eleven.
    The word is **vehicle**.
    *The **vehicle** needed repairing urgently.*
    The word is **vehicle**.

12. Spelling twelve.
    The word is **difference**.
    *There's a **difference** between winning and losing.*
    The word is **difference**.

At the end of the test, read out **all 12** sentences again, and give the children time to change their answers if they want to.
When the test is over, say "This is the end of the test."

© CGP — not to be photocopied

Set B: Spelling Questions

> Read out the instructions from the **first page** of this pull-out. Then read out the following:

1. Spelling one.
   The word is **older**.
   *Anna wants to be a pilot when she is **older**.*
   The word is **older**.

2. Spelling two.
   The word is **uneven**.
   *The ground was very **uneven**.*
   The word is **uneven**.

3. Spelling three.
   The word is **pressure**.
   *People can feel under **pressure** during exams.*
   The word is **pressure**.

4. Spelling four.
   The word is **tiniest**.
   *Mushtaq has the **tiniest** little dog.*
   The word is **tiniest**.

5. Spelling five.
   The word is **popping**.
   *The corks made a **popping** noise when they came out of the bottles.*
   The word is **popping**.

6. Spelling six.
   The word is **gracious**.
   *He was a very **gracious** host.*
   The word is **gracious**.

7. Spelling seven.
   The word is **myth**.
   *The Greek **myth** was popular with the children.*
   The word is **myth**.

8. Spelling eight.
   The word is **offering**.
   *Sam had been **offering** to help all day.*
   The word is **offering**.

9. Spelling nine.
   The word is **society**.
   *Today's **society** relies a lot on computers.*
   The word is **society**.

10. Spelling ten.
    The word is **official**.
    *The **official** document got lost in the post.*
    The word is **official**.

11. Spelling eleven.
    The word is **vague**.
    *Arran's instructions were too **vague**.*
    The word is **vague**.

12. Spelling twelve.
    The word is **advised**.
    *He **advised** against selling the house.*
    The word is **advised**.

> At the end of the test, read out **all 12** sentences again, and give the children time to change their answers if they want to.
> When the test is over, say "This is the end of the test."

© CGP — not to be photocopied

Set C: Spelling Questions

Read out the instructions from the **first page** of this pull-out. Then read out the following:

1. Spelling one.
   The word is **loaves**.
   *There were five **loaves** of bread in the cupboard.*
   The word is **loaves**.

2. Spelling two.
   The word is **prickly**.
   *The hedge was full of **prickly** thorns.*
   The word is **prickly**.

3. Spelling three.
   The word is **return**.
   *Chris thought a **return** journey was very unlikely.*
   The word is **return**.

4. Spelling four.
   The word is **obey**.
   *It was a rule to **obey** the sergeant at all times.*
   The word is **obey**.

5. Spelling five.
   The word is **microwave**.
   *It will be quickest to cook it in the **microwave**.*
   The word is **microwave**.

6. Spelling six.
   The word is **independent**.
   *Sarah was a very **independent** learner.*
   The word is **independent**.

7. Spelling seven.
   The word is **famous**.
   *The **famous** comedian signed lots of autographs.*
   The word is **famous**.

8. Spelling eight.
   The word is **impossible**.
   *He knew it was **impossible** to arrive on time.*
   The word is **impossible**.

9. Spelling nine.
   The word is **donation**.
   *The charitable **donation** was gratefully accepted.*
   The word is **donation**.

10. Spelling ten.
    The word is **scissors**.
    *It is important to carry **scissors** safely.*
    The word is **scissors**.

11. Spelling eleven.
    The word is **enough**.
    *Her mother said there was not **enough** milk.*
    The word is **enough**.

12. Spelling twelve.
    The word is **secretary**.
    *The teacher spoke to the school **secretary**.*
    The word is **secretary**.

At the end of the test, read out **all 12** sentences again, and give the children time to change their answers if they want to.

When the test is over, say "This is the end of the test."

© CGP — not to be photocopied

7. Read the two sentences below. Explain how the meaning of the sentence is changed when the **comma** is added.

Jessica loves bacon sandwiches and boiled eggs.

Jessica loves bacon, sandwiches and boiled eggs.

....

....

1 mark

8. Read the sentences below and circle the **determiner** in each one.

We travelled the distance between London and Dover .

Rory's golf ball is lime green .

There was an unusual squeaking sound .

1 mark

9. Look at the table below. Put a tick in each row to show whether each apostrophe is used as a **possessive** apostrophe or to create a **contracted form**.

Sentence	Possessive Apostrophe	Contracted Form
Makayla's car is white.		
The horses' manes are smooth.		
I can't go to the concert.		

1 mark

10. The sentence below is missing a **hyphen**.
Tick one box to show where the hyphen should go.

Swimmers ran out of the water due to a man eating shark.
☐ ☐ ☐ ☐

1 mark

11. Read the sentences below. Change all the underlined verbs from the **present** tense to the **past** tense.

One has already been done for you.

Frances <u>is</u> pleased that her new car <u>has</u> air conditioning.

| was | |

Harriet's dog <u>plays</u> with its toys and <u>chases</u> next door's cat.

| | |

The Johnsons <u>fly</u> to Nepal on Saturday.

| |

2 marks

END OF TEST

/ 12

Set B: Spelling Test

For this test, you'll need someone to **read out** the transcript from the middle of the book, or you can use the **online audio file**. The test will take about 10 minutes.

mark box

1. Anna wants to be a pilot when she is ....

2. The ground was very ....

3. People can feel under .... during exams.

4. Mushtaq has the .... little dog.

5. The corks made a .... noise when they came out of the bottles.

6. He was a very .... host.

7. The Greek .... was popular with the children.

8. Sam had been .... to help all day.

9. Today's .... relies a lot on computers.

10. The .... document got lost in the post.

11. Arran's instructions were too ....

12. He .... against selling the house.

/ 12

Set B: Puzzle

This puzzle is a brilliant way to practise your spelling skills.

Dinosaur Directions

Dan the Dinosaur has invited you to a secret picnic. He's given you a set of directions, but you should only use the ones that are spelt correctly. Start at the point shown by the arrow and follow the correct directions along the dotted paths. Mark the picnic spot with an X on the map and underline the spelling mistakes in the directions you didn't follow.

1. Head north, passing two volcanoes.
2. Turn right and cross the brigde.
3. At the bakery, turn east and go along the path until you reach a tree.
4. Cross the stream and go east at the second spaceship.
5. Turn north after the tree and carry on until you see a line of volcanos.
6. Follow the east side off the stream until you get to a bridge.
7. Go through the gate and turn south just before you reach the crater.
8. Follow the west side of the stream untill you reach the bridge.
9. Cross the bridge and continue passed the spaceship to the gate.
10. Walk until you reach the volcano. Then go south and head to the crater. You've found the picnic spot!

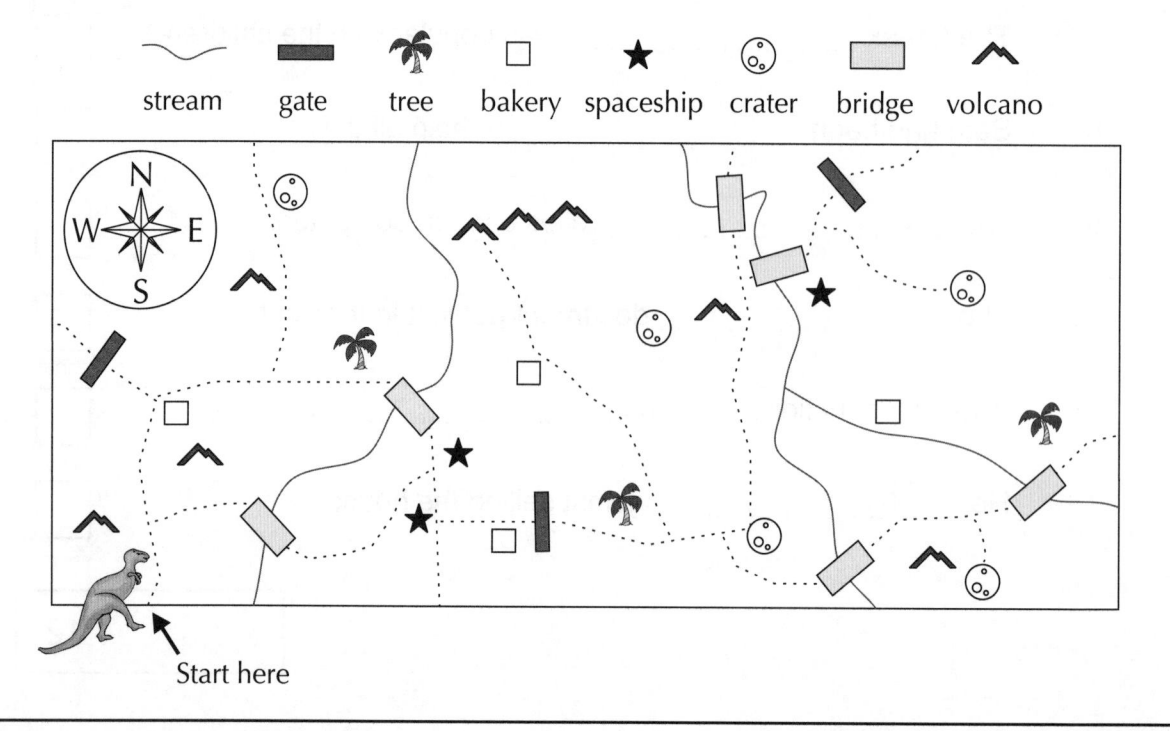

stream   gate   tree   bakery   spaceship   crater   bridge   volcano

Start here

Set B: Puzzle

38

© CGP — not to be photocopied

End of Set B: Scoresheet

You've finished a full set of tests — well done!

Now it's time to put your scores in here
and see how you're getting on.

	Score	
Test 1		/12
Test 2		/12
Test 3		/12
Test 4		/12
Spelling Test		/12
Total		/60

Once you've got a score out of 60, check it out in the table below...

0 – 29	If you got a lot of questions wrong, don't worry. Ask an adult to help you work out the **areas** you need **more practice** on. Then have another go at **this** set of tests.
30 – 45	If you got half-marks or better, you're doing well. **Read** back over your **incorrect** answers and make sure you know **why** they're wrong. Then try the **next set** of tests.
46 – 60	Woohoo! Now have a go at the **next set** of tests — can you beat your score?

But before you do... bend your brain round this one:

Add another comma to this sentence to save Granny's life.

The children shouted, "Let's eat Granny!"

Set C: Grammar & Punctuation 1

There are **12 questions** in this test. Give yourself **10 minutes** to answer them all.

1. Read the sentence below.
   Circle the most suitable **pronoun** to complete the sentence.

   When I arrive, I will show .... the map.

   hers   you   he   mine

   1 mark

2. Read the sentence below and circle the **adjective**.

   Molly found her favourite teddy beneath the bed.

   1 mark

3. Read the sentences below.
   Tick the sentence which uses a **colon** correctly.

   tick **one** box

   My friends are twins their names are Rose: and Scott. ☐
   My friends: are twins their names are Rose and Scott. ☐
   My friends are twins: their names are Rose and Scott. ☐
   My friends are: twins their names are Rose and Scott. ☐

   1 mark

4. Read the sentence below and underline the **conjunction**.

While you're waiting, you can read a magazine.

1 mark

5. Read the words below.
Tick the words that are **antonyms** for 'open'.

tick **one** box

easy, simple ☐
shut, blocked ☐
clear, accessible ☐
imprisoned, captive ☐

1 mark

6. The words below are part of a **word family**.
Write **one** other word that belongs to this word family in the box.

deceive   perceive   conceive

☐

1 mark

7. Read the sentence below and underline the words which should start with a **capital letter**.

tomorrow is my birthday so i am going to liverpool

1 mark

8. Read the sentences below.
   Tick **two** sentences which should end with a **question mark**.

	tick **two** boxes
Ask your father where he's put my glasses	☐
What I needed to do has now been done	☐
That's where your uncle lives, isn't it	☐
What a wonderful surprise	☐
You'd like an apple, wouldn't you	☐

   1 mark

9. Put a tick in each row to show whether '**until**' is being used as a **subordinating conjunction** or a **preposition**.

Sentence	Preposition	Subordinating conjunction
They didn't stop laughing **until** the end of the film.		
Until I went to America, I had never travelled outside of Europe.		
I couldn't speak Italian **until** I began to have lessons.		

   1 mark

10. Put a prefix at the start of each word below to make it mean the **opposite**.

    .... possible

    .... helpful

    .... sane

    1 mark

11. In the sentences below, **underline** the co-ordinating conjunction(s) and **circle** the subordinating conjunction(s).

I was running (because) I was late.

I'm allergic to coconuts <u>but</u> not to peanuts.

I tripped <u>and</u> twisted my ankle.

1 mark

12. Put a tick in the correct column to show whether each sentence is **active** or **passive**. One has already been done for you.

Sentence	Active	Passive
The parcel was sent to the wrong address.		✓
The crowd cheered the athletes.		
They took the cakes round to Mrs Beeton.		
The hospital was opened by the mayor.		

1 mark

END OF TEST

/ 12

Set C: Grammar & Punctuation 2

There are **11 questions** in this test. Give yourself **10 minutes** to answer them all.

1. The sentence below is missing two **commas**.
   Tick **two** boxes to show where the commas should go.

   I have three cats one dog two rabbits and a hamster.
   ↑ ↑ ↑ ↑
   □ □ □ □

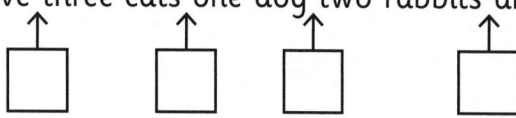

   1 mark

2. Read the sentences below.
   Tick the sentence that is a **command**.

   tick **one** box

   Where has Mr Patel gone? □

   This game is so cool! □

   Take the dog for a walk. □

   Natalie loves her ballet classes. □

   1 mark

3. Read the sentence below and circle the **adverb**.

   The witch flew swiftly towards the hidden forest.

   1 mark

Set C: Grammar & Punctuation 2

4. Draw a line to match each word below with a **synonym**.
   One has already been done for you.

   mundane — request
   loyal — boring
   appeal — devoted

   (appeal is linked to request)

   1 mark

5. The sentences in the table are missing either '**a**' or '**an**'.
   Put a tick in the right column for each one.

	a	an
For dessert we made .... apple crumble.		
I hope I get .... new jumper for Christmas.		
Alphonsa has .... green P.E. bag.		

   1 mark

6. Read the sentences below.
   Tick the sentence which uses **dashes** correctly.

   tick **one** box

   I hope Tia is — feeling better she was off school today. ☐
   I hope Tia is feeling better she was off — school today. ☐
   I hope — Tia is feeling better she was off school today. ☐
   I hope Tia is feeling better — she was off school today. ☐

   1 mark

7. Read the passage below. Change all the underlined verbs from the **present** tense to the **past** tense.
One has already been done for you.

My brother <u>plays</u> for a local football team.
↑
| **played** |

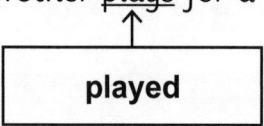

On Saturdays, I <u>watch</u> his matches.
↑
| |

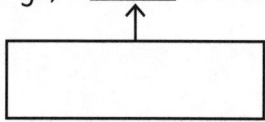

Football <u>is</u> one of my hobbies as well.
↑
| |

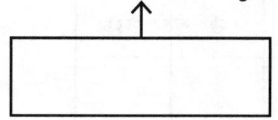

I <u>buy</u> football stickers and <u>keep</u> them in a folder.
↑   ↑
| | | |

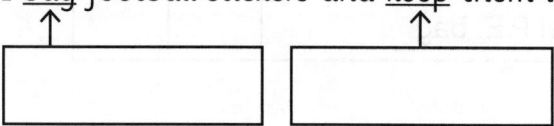

2 marks

8. Underline the **modal verbs** in the sentences below.

There should be more ice cream in the freezer.

I would walk the dog if you asked me to.

1 mark

9. Each sentence below is missing an **apostrophe**. Add in the apostrophes in the correct places.

   Rasheed's mum is a firefighter.

   Heather's cats were very sleepy.

   The fairies' home is in that tree.

   1 mark

10. Tick the sentences that contain a **preposition**.

The cat is sleeping under the table.	☐
See me before you leave.	☐
I had to leave during the performance.	☐
Until it stops raining, we should play inside.	☐

    1 mark

11. Read the sentence below.
    What is '**which is on the south coast**' an example of?

    Brighton, which is on the south coast, is a lovely place.

    tick **one** box

a conjunction	☐
a main clause	☐
a relative clause	☐
a noun phrase	☐

    1 mark

END OF TEST

/ 12

Set C: Grammar & Punctuation 3

There are **11 questions** in this test. Give yourself **10 minutes** to answer them all.

1. Read the sentence below and underline all the **pronouns**.

    She asked if it was yours or mine.

    1 mark

2. Look at the table below. Change the question into a **statement**. Write the statement in the right-hand column.

Question	Statement
Is jam the best sandwich filling?	

    1 mark

3. The <u>pirate</u> <u>ran</u> as fast as his wooden leg could <u>carry</u> him.

    In each row, put a tick to show whether each underlined word is a **verb** or a **noun**.

Word	Verb	Noun
pirate		
ran		
carry		

    1 mark

4. Read the sentences below.
Tick the sentence that uses **dashes** correctly.

tick **one** box

My new — dog — a golden retriever is called Rover. ☐

My new dog — a golden retriever — is called Rover. ☐

My new dog a golden retriever — is called Rover. ☐

1 mark

5. Read the sentence below and circle all the **determiners**.

Twenty children ran through both doors into the hall.

1 mark

6. The words below are part of a **word family**.
Write **one** other word that belongs to this word family in the box.

literature   illiterate   alliteration

1 mark

7. The doctor said I should get plenty of rest.

   Rewrite the sentence above so that the doctor's words are in **direct speech**.

   ....

   ....

   2 marks

8. Read the sentence below, then tick the option that completes the sentence so that it uses the **subjunctive mood**.

   It is essential that he .... the plant each day.

   tick **one** box

   waters ☐
   water ☐
   watering ☐
   watered ☐

   1 mark

9. Read the sentence below and underline the **subject**.

   Lucy showed Meera around the school.

   1 mark

10. Read the sentences below.
Tick the sentence which uses a **semi-colon** correctly.

tick **one** box

Rama; is a boy Sita is a girl. ☐

Rama is a boy Sita; is a girl. ☐

Rama is a boy Sita is; a girl. ☐

Rama is a boy; Sita is a girl. ☐

1 mark

11. Read the information in the box below. Write one sentence that lists all this information. Make sure you use correct punctuation.

Meal Deal
ham sandwich
prawn cocktail crisps
banana
drink (still or fizzy)

....

....

1 mark

END OF TEST

/ 12

Set C: Grammar & Punctuation 4

There are **11 questions** in this test. Give yourself **10 minutes** to answer them all.

1. Read the sentences below. Circle the correct form of the verb in brackets to complete each sentence in the **present perfect** form.

   Anita (has seen / saw) the film.

   The boys (were / have been) on time all week.

   The hen (has gone / went) into the barn.

   1 mark

2. Read the sentences below. Tick the **two** sentences which are **formal**.

   tick **two** boxes

   Paul and I would appreciate a lift home. ☐

   I've been to the new shop that's just opened. ☐

   I would be grateful if you could help me. ☐

   None of the monkeys escaped, did they? ☐

   1 mark

3. The passage below contains **commands**. Circle the **two** words which show this.

Mix the ingredients together in a large bowl. Next, you will need to get two small tins ready to bake the cake. Pour the mixture into the tins evenly.

1 mark

4. Read the sentence below. Insert **two commas** so that the sentence is punctuated correctly.

My mum who is a great baker owns the cake shop in town.

1 mark

5. Tick **two** boxes to show which of the words in the sentence below are **co-ordinating conjunctions**.

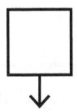

The wedding was in a church, and started at two o'clock, but the reception was at a local hotel.

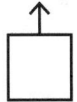

1 mark

6. Write a **question** beginning with the word given below.

   Where ....

   ....

   1 mark

7. Read the sentences below.
   Tick the **preposition** that best completes **both** sentences.

   I've spilt juice down the front .... my shirt.

   It was nice .... you to offer.

   tick **one** box

   of   ☐
   on   ☐
   about   ☐
   from   ☐

   1 mark

8. Complete the sentence below with an **adjective** formed from the noun in the box.

   critic
   ↓

   Mr Barnes is a _____ teacher who's

   always telling us off.

   1 mark

9. Read the sentence below.
   Underline the longest possible noun phrase.

   Kim wants to be a famous professional gymnast one day.

   1 mark

10. Rewrite the sentence below with the **adverbial** at the beginning.
    Make sure you use the same words and the correct punctuation.

    Do the extra questions on page one when you've finished.

    ....

    ....

    1 mark

11. The sentences below are each missing a **colon**.
    Tick **one** box for each sentence to show where the colon should go.

    The teddy bear was very old it had belonged to Sara's mother.

    Zena had three cats Smokey, Poppy and Scout.

    2 marks

END OF TEST

/ 12

Set C: Spelling Test

For this test, you'll need someone to **read out** the transcript from the middle of the book, or you can use the **online audio file**. The test will take about 10 minutes.

mark box

1. There were five .... of bread in the cupboard. ☐

2. The hedge was full of .... thorns. ☐

3. Chris thought a .... journey was very unlikely. ☐

4. It was a rule to .... the sergeant at all times. ☐

5. It will be quickest to cook it in the .... ☐

6. Sarah was a very .... learner. ☐

7. The .... comedian signed lots of autographs. ☐

8. He knew it was .... to arrive on time. ☐

9. The charitable .... was gratefully accepted. ☐

10. It is important to carry .... safely. ☐

11. Her mother said there was not .... milk. ☐

12. The teacher spoke to the school .... ☐

/ 12

Set C: Puzzle

This puzzle is a brilliant way to practise your grammar skills.

Football Fears

The passage below is missing some verbs. Find ten verbs in the word search — the hidden words could be written forwards, backwards or diagonally. Then use these verbs to complete the passage by writing them in the correct gaps.

```
B E I F R L T M J D K
A O L A G N I L E E F
L E F N S R Y S U L T
L W C S M I B O M E R
P L A Y I X B M A E I
L E H E L I D R J H P
D D E V E I L E B W P
E W C P D L Y M A T E
G V N M I S S E D R D
D W A R M I N G F A G
Y T H G E D E R O C S
```

Kelsey's team were about to ▢▢▢▢ a football match against their enemies from Thornywood Academy. Kelsey was ▢▢▢▢▢▢▢ very nervous. Last match, she had ▢▢▢▢▢▢▢ over and ▢▢▢▢▢▢ an important goal.

The coach ▢▢▢▢▢▢ at Kelsey as she was ▢▢▢▢▢▢▢ up. "Don't worry, Kelsey. You'll be great!" she said.

Kelsey hadn't ▢▢▢▢▢▢▢▢ her, but the coach was right — Kelsey ▢▢▢▢▢▢ two goals! Her teammates ▢▢▢▢ her high fives and she even ▢▢▢▢▢▢▢▢▢▢ across the pitch in celebration.

End of Set C: Scoresheet

You've finished a full set of tests — well done!

Now it's time to put your scores in here
and see how you're getting on.

	Score	
Test 1		/12
Test 2		/12
Test 3		/12
Test 4		/12
Spelling Test		/12
Total		**/60**

Once you've got a score out of 60, check it out in the table below...

0 – 29	If you got a lot of questions wrong, don't worry. Ask an adult to help you work out the **areas** you need **more practice** on. Then have another go at **this** set of tests.
30 – 45	If you got half-marks or better, you're doing well. **Read** back over your **incorrect** answers and make sure you know **why** they're wrong.
46 – 60	Woohoo! You've done really well — congratulations!

One last thing... bend your brain round this one:

Can you find the nine letter word hidden in the box? You can only use each letter once.

a   r   r   o   a
b   ~~e~~   d   ~~e~~

The word is c _ _ _ _ _ _ _ d .

Set C: Scoresheet

Hints and Tips

*Grammar, punctuation and spelling can be a bit tricky.
If you get stuck, this page might help you out.*

1. **Learn** the **main parts** of speech.

    The <u>teacher</u> <u>explained</u> the <u>difficult</u> topic.

    Noun   **Verb**   **Adjective**
    (a naming word)   (a doing or being word)   (a describing word)

2. Make sure you can identify the different **parts** of a **sentence**.

    <u>I think the boat leaves at six</u>, <u>although I'm not sure</u>.

    Main Clause   **Subordinate Clause**
    (the most important clause)   (the less important clause)

3. Always use **capital letters** for proper nouns and after **full stops**, **exclamation marks** and **question marks**.

    Proper noun

    We're leaving. Do we have to? Yes, David, right now!

    Capital letter   **Full stop**   **Question mark**   **Exclamation mark**

4. **Apostrophes** show **missing letters**, or that something **belongs** to someone.

    He's over there.   my dad's suitcase
    (This is a **contracted form** of 'he is'.)   (This is to show **possession**.)

5. **Break** words down into **smaller parts** to help you spell them.
    e.g.   dis-cov-ery   re-mem-ber-ing   in-ter-est-ed

Answers

Set A

Test 1 – Pages 2-5

1. We will go to the cinema tonight. (**1 mark**)

2. had (**1 mark**)

3. We cooked curry for tea, and we baked a cake for dessert.
   They will tell us a story, and we will listen carefully.
   (**1 mark for both correct**)

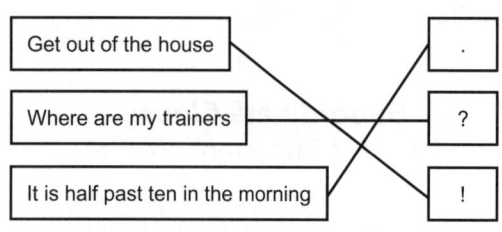

4.
   - Get out of the house → !
   - Where are my trainers → ?
   - It is half past ten in the morning → .

   (**1 mark for all three correct**)

5. He used to love those sour sweets.
   D   A   C   B
   (**1 mark for all four correct**)

6. Even after all this time, I still don't like cabbage. (**1 mark**)

7. Answers may vary, for example:

Word	Synonym	Antonym
intelligent	clever	foolish
optimistic	positive, hopeful, confident	pessimistic
courteous	polite	rude, impolite, cheeky
vibrant	lively	dull, boring

   (**1 mark for two correct, 2 marks for all three correct**)

8. <u>Although</u> it is really late, I can't get to sleep. (**1 mark**)

9. never (**1 mark**)

10. The teacher asked his pupils, "Is Marcus ill today?" (**1 mark**)

11.

Sentence	Main clause	Subordinate clause
When Ryan arrives tomorrow, we'll go to the cinema.		✓
Dad says that if we're good, **we can buy some popcorn**.	✓	
Ryan, who's my cousin, loves popcorn.		✓

(**1 mark for all three correct**)

Test 2 – Pages 6-9

1. We went outside <u>after</u> it had stopped raining.

   I'm not going to the party <u>unless</u> Naomi comes with me.

   <u>Whenever</u> Jimmy's dog barks, his cat hides under the bed.
   (**1 mark for all three correct**)

2. am eating (**1 mark**)

3. The alarm was ignored by the children. (**1 mark**)

4. Graham (my uncle) loves smoked salmon. (**1 mark**)

5. a pastry (**1 mark**)

6. The woman, who was very tall, had ✓ forgotten to bring her screwdriver, which ✓ meant she couldn't hang up our pictures.
   (**1 mark for both correct**)

7. cheerful (**1 mark**)

8. forcefully (**1 mark**)

Answers

9. In our garage, there's a <u>brightly coloured, ultrafast sports car</u>. (**1 mark**)

10. I don't eat tomatoes <u>unless they're cooked</u>. (**1 mark**)

11. a) dads, isnt, Im
    (**1 mark for all three correct**)

    b) Possible answers:
    dad's — to show possession
    isn't — to show that a letter is missing
    I'm — to show that a letter is missing
    (**1 mark**)

Test 3 – Pages 10-13

1. Whose, your, an, every
   (**1 mark for all four correct**)

2. What an incredible goal that was
   Get out of my way
   (**1 mark for both correct**)

3. Tomek <u>was</u> the best at playing the recorder.

   We <u>were</u> allowed to meet the band backstage.

   I <u>was</u> doing my homework when he arrived.
   (**1 mark for all three correct**)

4. For the experiment, Nicola will need:
   • a microwave
   • a thermometer
   • a bar of chocolate
   (**1 mark for any answer with <u>consistent</u> punctuation and capitalisation, as above**)

Answers with commas or semi-colons after each of the first two items and a full stop after the third are also acceptable. The use of a capital letter at the start of every item is also acceptable.

5. Amar met Laura, <u>who is now his best friend</u>, last July. (**1 mark**)

6. this term (**1 mark**)

7. Mum found the car keys — they were in her pocket. (**1 mark**)

8. probably, soon
   (**1 mark for both correct**)

9. hundred (**1 mark**)

10. Marie is in hospital ↑✓ she's having an operation. (**1 mark**)

11. Answers may vary, for example:

Question	Answer
Where do you live?	At 42 Lime Tree Avenue.
What did you have for lunch?	A sandwich and a banana.
What time does school start?	At quarter to nine.

(**1 mark for each appropriate question with correct punctuation**)

Answers

Test 4 – Pages 14-17

1. are you (**1 mark**)
2.

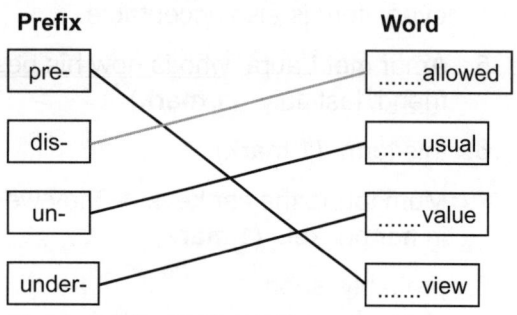

Prefix	Word
pre-	......allowed
dis-	......usual
un-	......value
under-	......view

   pre- → view
   dis- → allowed
   un- → usual
   under- → value

   (**1 mark for all three correct**)

3. Everyone's costumes are over there.
   (**1 mark**)

4. Yasmin offered me a sweet.
   My favourite colour is orange.
   (**1 mark for both correct**)

5. The speaker is talking to Jane in the first sentence, but to somebody else in the second sentence. (**1 mark**)

6. I lost the board game <u>before</u> I lost at cards, <u>but</u> it didn't matter <u>because</u> I won at chess. (**1 mark for all three correct**)

7. I heard you were ill are you feeling better? (**1 mark**)

8. that (**1 mark**)

9. cold, chilly, cool
   (**1 mark for any suitable word, as above**)

10. Last night, Jacob's dad bought us all pizza. (**1 mark**)

11. hasn't, has not
    (**1 mark for either of the above**)

12.

Sentence	Active	Passive
Everyone loved watching sports day.	✓	
I was driven here by my mum.		✓
I can grow fruit and vegetables.	✓	
We were shown round by the tour guide.		✓

(**1 mark for all three correct**)

Spelling Test – Page 18

For full sentence answers, see the pull-out transcripts in the middle of the book.

1. mixture (**1 mark**)
2. sadly (**1 mark**)
3. running (**1 mark**)
4. disorder (**1 mark**)
5. houses (**1 mark**)
6. stomach (**1 mark**)
7. relief (**1 mark**)
8. doubt (**1 mark**)
9. delicious (**1 mark**)
10. thought (**1 mark**)
11. vehicle (**1 mark**)
12. difference (**1 mark**)

Answers

Puzzle – Page 19

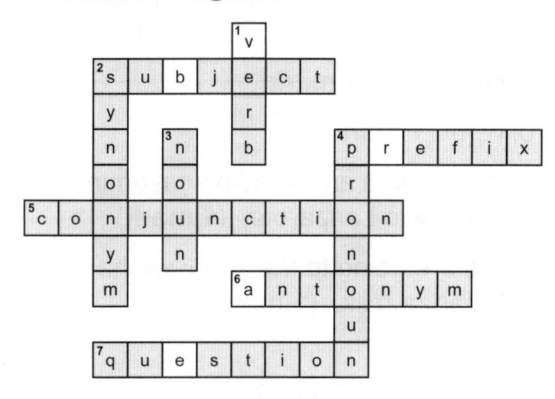

Crossword answers:
- 1 down: verb
- 2 across: subject
- 2 down: synonym
- 3 down: noun
- 4 down: pronoun
- 4 across: prefix
- 5 across: conjunction
- 6 across: antonym
- 7 across: question

Paige's favourite type of word is an adverb.

Scoresheet Question – Page 20

LOSE   LONE

Set B

Test 1 – Pages 21-24

1. was packing, was looking (**1 mark**)

2. a) Theres, Lucys, Ill
   (**1 mark for all three correct**)

   b) Possible answers:
   There's — to show that a letter is missing
   Lucy's — to show possession
   I'll — to show that letters are missing
   (**1 mark**)

3. When his sister was born, Vince was five years old. (**1 mark**)

4. Answers may vary, for example:
   Tell me the truth. (**1 mark**)

5. because (**1 mark**)

6. Mr Hargreaves (our history teacher) rides a motorbike to school.
   My dress (the red one) has got a stain on it.
   (**1 mark for both correct**)

7. extra, additional
   (**1 mark for both correct**)

8. Melanie carefully put the dishes in the ✓ dishwasher after dinner. ✓
   (**1 mark for both correct**)

9. Last Saturday, I went to Manchester and saw a show. (**1 mark**)

10.

Sentence	Certainty	Possibility
Julie will write a letter to her brother.	✓	
I may see Thomas next Tuesday.		✓
He should see a doctor about his leg.	✓	
We might go on holiday to Florida.		✓

(**1 mark for all four correct**)

11. If I were you, I'd wear shorts and a T-shirt. (**1 mark**)

Test 2 – Pages 25-28

1. <u>Lydia</u> found a beautiful necklace.
   Last week, <u>I</u> played football in the park.
   At 9 o'clock, <u>the postman</u> delivered the letters. (**1 mark for all three correct**)

2. Patrick is good at cricket (and) tennis <u>although</u> he doesn't play very often.
   (**1 mark**)

Answers

3. You may choose from these three desserts:
   - chocolate pudding
   - fruit tart
   - ice cream

   (**1 mark for any answer with consistent punctuation and capitalisation, as above**)

   Answers with commas or semi-colons after each of the first two items and a full stop after the third are also acceptable. The use of a capital letter at the start of every item is also acceptable.

4.

Word	Adjective	Adverb
ever		✓
large	✓	
pink	✓	

   (**1 mark for all three correct**)

5. do they (**1 mark**)

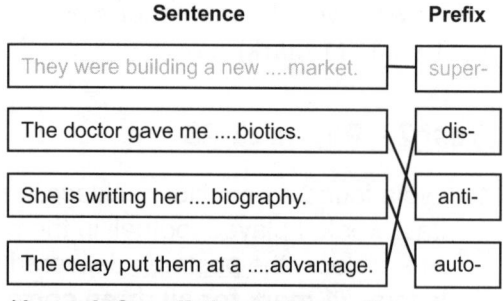

6.
Sentence	Prefix
They were building a new ....market.	super-
The doctor gave me ....biotics.	dis-
She is writing her ....biography.	anti-
The delay put them at a ....advantage.	auto-

   (**1 mark for all three correct**)

7. I have told him the truth.
   A flea has bitten my dog.
   (**1 mark for both correct**)

8. I can't believe it, we've won the competition (**1 mark**)

9. Ralph has just bought a big red and ↑✓ shiny car. (**1 mark**)

10. verb (**1 mark**)

11. We booked an incredible <u>last-minute</u> holiday to Lanzarote. (**1 mark**)

12. We are going to the shop: we have no bread or milk. (**1 mark**)

Test 3 – Pages 29-32

1. al (**1 mark**)

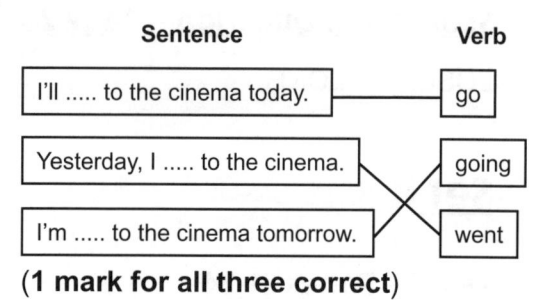

2.
Sentence	Verb
I'll ..... to the cinema today.	go
Yesterday, I ..... to the cinema.	going
I'm ..... to the cinema tomorrow.	went

   (lines cross: today→go, yesterday→went, tomorrow→going)

   (**1 mark for all three correct**)

3. mine (**1 mark**)

4. Which jumper are you going to wear today (**1 mark**)

5. "What were you thinking?" asked the chef. "You can't make meringue with lavender!" (**1 mark**)

6. Sarah looked at me she could tell ↑✓ I wasn't joking. (**1 mark**)

7. Lewis found a famous painting last week. (**1 mark**)

8. were (**1 mark**)

Answers

9. The cloud, which was dark grey, was ↑✓ directly above Fred, who wasn't ↑✓ wearing a raincoat.
   (**1 mark for both correct**)

10. he, I (**1 mark**)

11. Answers may vary, for example:

    We always drive to the swimming baths. Mum is parking the car on the drive.
    (**1 mark for one correct, 2 marks for both correct**)

Test 4 – Pages 33-36

1. apologise (**1 mark**)

2. Answers may vary, for example:

   What film shall we watch tonight?
   (**1 mark**)

3. are balancing, are throwing (**1 mark**)

4. The prisoner was captured.
   Our decision was made.
   (**1 mark for both correct**)

5. I missed the parade the one on ↑✓ High Street because I overslept. ↑✓
   (**1 mark for both correct**)

6. while (**1 mark**)

7. When the comma is added, bacon sandwiches become two separate things — bacon and sandwiches.
   (**1 mark**)

8. We travelled <u>the</u> distance between London and Dover.
   <u>Rory's</u> golf ball is lime green.
   There was <u>an</u> unusual squeaking sound.
   (**1 mark for all three correct**)

9.
Sentence	Possessive Apostrophe	Contracted Form
Makayla's car is white.	✓	
The horses' manes are smooth.	✓	
I can't go to the concert.		✓

   (**1 mark for all three correct**)

10. Swimmers ran out of the water due to a man eating shark.
    ↑✓
    (**1 mark**)

11. has — had
    plays — played
    chases — chased
    fly — flew
    (**1 mark for two or three correct, 2 marks for all four correct**)

Spelling Test – Page 37

For full sentence answers, see the pull-out transcripts in the middle of the book.

1. older (**1 mark**)
2. uneven (**1 mark**)
3. pressure (**1 mark**)
4. tiniest (**1 mark**)
5. popping (**1 mark**)
6. gracious (**1 mark**)
7. myth (**1 mark**)
8. offering (**1 mark**)

Answers

9. society (**1 mark**)
10. official (**1 mark**)
11. vague (**1 mark**)
12. advised (**1 mark**)

Puzzle – Page 38

You should have underlined:

1. Head north, passing two volcanoes.
2. Turn right and cross the <u>brigde</u>.
3. At the bakery, turn east and go along the path until you reach a tree.
4. Cross the stream and go east at the second spaceship.
5. Turn north after the tree and carry on until you see a line of <u>volcanos</u>.
6. Follow the east side <u>off</u> the stream until you get to a bridge.
7. Go through the gate and turn south just before you reach the crater.
8. Follow the west side of the stream <u>untill</u> you reach the bridge.
9. Cross the bridge and continue <u>passed</u> the spaceship to the gate.
10. Walk until you reach the volcano. Then go south and head to the crater. You've found the picnic spot!

You should have followed directions 1, 3, 4, 7 & 10, which led to the secret picnic spot marked with an X below:

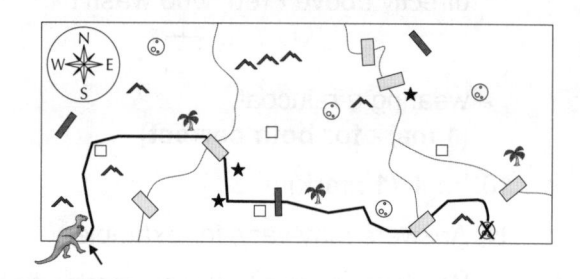

Scoresheet Question – Page 39

The children shouted, "Let's eat, Granny!"

Set C

Test 1 – Pages 40-43

1. you (**1 mark**)
2. favourite (**1 mark**)
3. My friends are twins: their names are Rose and Scott. (**1 mark**)
4. <u>While</u> you're waiting, you can read a magazine. (**1 mark**)
5. shut, blocked (**1 mark**)
6. receive, deceived
   (**1 mark for any answer with the root word 'ceive', as above**)
7. <u>tomorrow</u> is my birthday so <u>i</u> am going to <u>liverpool</u>.
   (**1 mark for all three correct**)
8. That's where your uncle lives, isn't it
   You'd like an apple, wouldn't you
   (**1 mark for both correct**)

Answers

Answers

9.

Sentence	Preposition	Subordinating conjunction
They didn't stop laughing **until** the end of the film.	✓	
Until I went to America, I had never travelled outside of Europe.		✓
I couldn't speak Italian **until** I began to have lessons.		✓

(**1 mark for all three correct**)

10. impossible, unhelpful, insane
    (**1 mark for all three correct**)

11. I was running (because) I was late.
    I'm allergic to coconuts <u>but</u> not to peanuts.
    I tripped <u>and</u> twisted my ankle.
    (**1 mark for all three correct**)

12.

Sentence	Active	Passive
The parcel was sent to the wrong address.		✓
The crowd cheered the athletes.	✓	
They took the cakes round to Mrs Beeton.	✓	
The hospital was opened by the mayor.		✓

(**1 mark for all three correct**)

Test 2 – Pages 44-47

1. I have three cats one dog two rabbits
   ✓ ✓
   and a hamster.
   (**1 mark for both correct**)

2. Take the dog for a walk. (**1 mark**)

3. swiftly (**1 mark**)

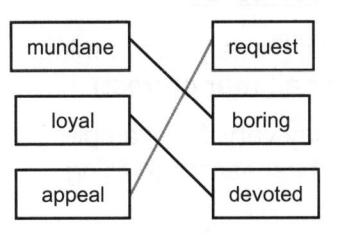

4. mundane — boring
   loyal — devoted
   appeal — request
   (**1 mark for both correct**)

5.

	a	an
For dessert we made ...... apple crumble.		✓
I hope I get ...... new jumper for Christmas.	✓	
Alphonsa has ...... green P.E. bag.	✓	

(**1 mark for all three correct**)

6. I hope Tia is feeling better — she was off school today. (**1 mark**)

7. watch — watched
   is — was
   buy — bought
   keep — kept
   (**1 mark for two or three correct, 2 marks for all four correct**)

8. should, would
   (**1 mark for both correct**)

9. Rasheed's mum is a firefighter.
   Heather's cats were very sleepy.
   The fairies' home is in that tree.
   (**1 mark for all three correct**)

10. The cat is sleeping under the table.
    I had to leave during the performance.
    (**1 mark for both correct**)

11. a relative clause (**1 mark**)

Answers

Test 3 – Pages 48-51

1. <u>She</u> asked if <u>it</u> was <u>yours</u> or <u>mine</u>.
   (**1 mark for all four correct**)

2. Answers may vary, for example:
   Jam is the best sandwich filling.
   (**1 mark**)

3.

Word	Verb	Noun
pirate		✓
ran	✓	
carry	✓	

   (**1 mark for all three correct**)

4. My new dog — a golden retriever — is called Rover. (**1 mark**)

5. Twenty, both, the
   (**1 mark for all three correct**)

6. literate, literacy, literally
   (**1 mark for any answer with the root word 'liter', as above**)

7. You should get plenty of rest
   (**1 mark for correct transformation of speech**)

   "You should get plenty of rest."
   (**1 further mark for correct punctuation**)

   Answers may or may not include attribution, e.g. said the doctor.

8. water (**1 mark**)

9. <u>Lucy</u> showed Meera around the school.
   (**1 mark**)

10. Rama is a boy; Sita is a girl. (**1 mark**)

11. In the meal deal, you get a ham sandwich, prawn cocktail crisps, a banana and a drink (still or fizzy).
    (**1 mark for any grammatically correct sentence which lists all of the information, as above**)

Test 4 – Pages 52-55

1. Anita <u>has seen</u> the film.
   The boys <u>have been</u> on time all week.
   The hen <u>has gone</u> into the barn.
   (**1 mark for all three correct**)

2. Paul and I would appreciate a lift home.
   I would be grateful if you could help me.
   (**1 mark for both correct**)

3. Mix, Pour
   (**1 mark for both correct**)

4. My mum, who is a great baker, owns the cake shop in town.
   (**1 mark for both correct**)

5. The wedding was in a church, and ↑✓ started at two o'clock, but the reception ↑✓ was at a local hotel.
   (**1 mark for both correct**)

6. Answers may vary, for example:
   Where is the police station? (**1 mark**)

7. of (**1 mark**)

8. critical (**1 mark**)

9. Kim wants to be <u>a famous professional gymnast</u> one day. (**1 mark**)

10. When you've finished, do the extra questions on page one. (**1 mark**)

Answers

11. The teddy bear was very old ↑[✓] it had belonged to Sara's mother.

    Zena had three cats ↑[✓] Smokey, Poppy and Scout.
    (**1 mark for one correct, 2 marks for both correct**)

Spelling Test – Page 56

For full sentence answers, see the pull-out transcripts in the middle of the book.

1. loaves (**1 mark**)
2. prickly (**1 mark**)
3. return (**1 mark**)
4. obey (**1 mark**)
5. microwave (**1 mark**)
6. independent (**1 mark**)
7. famous (**1 mark**)
8. impossible (**1 mark**)
9. donation (**1 mark**)
10. scissors (**1 mark**)
11. enough (**1 mark**)
12. secretary (**1 mark**)

Puzzle – Page 57

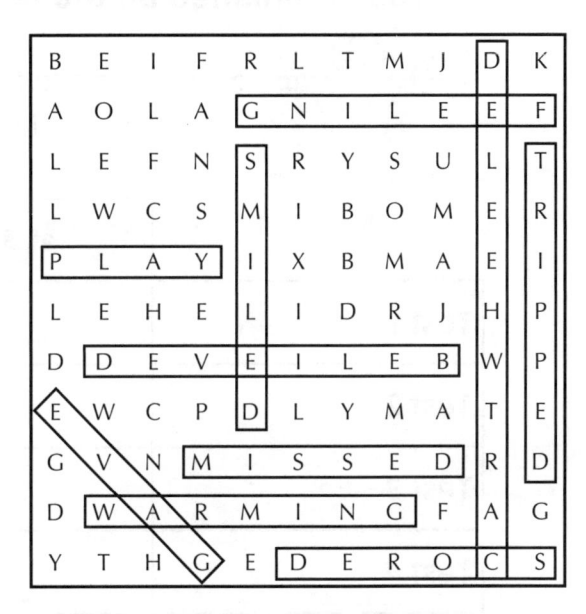

B	E	I	F	R	L	T	M	J	D	K
A	O	L	A	G	N	I	L	E	E	F
L	E	F	N	S	R	Y	S	U	L	T
L	W	C	S	M	I	B	O	M	E	R
P	L	A	Y	I	X	B	M	A	E	I
L	E	H	E	L	I	D	R	J	H	P
D	D	E	V	E	I	L	E	B	W	P
E	W	C	P	D	L	Y	M	A	T	E
G	V	N	M	I	S	S	E	D	R	D
D	W	A	R	M	I	N	G	F	A	G
Y	T	H	G	E	D	E	R	O	C	S

Kelsey's team were about to **play** a football match against their enemies from Thornywood Academy. Kelsey was **feeling** very nervous. Last match, she had **tripped** over and **missed** an important goal.

The coach **smiled** at Kelsey as she was **warming** up.
"Don't worry, Kelsey. You'll be great!" she said.
Kelsey hadn't **believed** her, but the coach was right — Kelsey **scored** two goals! Her teammates **gave** her high fives and she even **cartwheeled** across the pitch in celebration.

Scoresheet Question – Page 58

cardboard

Progress Chart

You've finished all the tests in the book — well done!

Now it's time to put your scores in here and see how you've done.

	Set A	Set B	Set C
Test 1			
Test 2			
Test 3			
Test 4			
Spelling Test			
Total			

See if you're on target by checking your marks for each set in the table below.

Mark	
0-29	You're not quite there yet, but don't worry — keep going back over the questions you find tricky and you'll improve your grammar, punctuation and spelling skills in no time.
30-45	Good job! You're doing really well, but make sure you keep working on your weaker topics so that you're really ready for your test.
46-60	Give yourself a huge pat on the back — you're on track to ace your test! You're a grammar, punctuation and spelling star!